MW00987815

How To

MAXIMIZE FEE$

In Professional Service Firms

**A Handbook for Professionals
In Consulting, Law, Finance, Architecture,
Real Estate And Other Personal Service Firms**

ALAN WEISS, PH.D.

author of
*Million Dollar Consulting:
The Professional's Guide to Growing A Practice*

How To
MAXIMIZE FEE$
In Professional Service Firms

**A Handbook for Professionals
In Consulting, Law, Finance, Architecture,
Real Estate And Other Personal Service Firms**

ALAN WEISS, PH.D.

Las Brisas Research Press

© 1994 Summit Consulting Group, Inc.

This book is copyrighted material. All rights are reserved.

It is against the law to make copies of this material without securing specific, written permission in advance from Summit Consulting Group, Inc.

No part of this publication may be reproduced, stored in retrieval systems, or transmitted in any form or by any means—including but not limited to electronic, mechanical, photocopying, and recording—without the prior written permission of the copyright holder.

Printed in the United States of America

Published by Las Brisas Research Press, East Greenwich, RI 02818

ISBN 0-910924-00-7

Table of Contents

Introduction

"There are 57 different keys for increasing fees you will review by the time you finish this brief booklet."

This book was written in response to the tremendously popular workshops I've conducted all around the country on pricing professional services. During more than 20 years in the consulting profession, I've observed the preponderance of my professional colleagues taking the inevitable risks that accompany such ventures, but generally failing to reap the rewards.

They consistently undervalue their own contributions to their clients' success.

As my professional speaking and consulting activities exposed me to architects, realtors, financial advisors, designers, attorneys, dentists, physicians, engineers and other professions, I found that such undervaluing was endemic to most of them. This is especially damaging for those operating as solo practitioners and in small firms, whether as principal or employee.

This handbook is intended as an inexpensive remedy. It is meant to provoke and to stimulate. You might disagree with its premises at times, or you might question as to how you could ever apply some of the approaches, particularly with a mortage payment due next month or a tuition bill in the mailbox. All I can tell you by way of assurance is that I use all of these techniques annually, and I make a million dollars doing it. Moreover, the people who have attended my workshops, heard my keynotes, listened to my cassettes and read my books have called and written attesting to the power of the ideas of basing fees on value, developing long-term relationships, and using proposals and contracts only to reaffirm previously-established conceptual agreement.

This is the first time these practices and principles have been placed in an inexpensive, easily-accessible medium.

Because people learn in different ways, and some readers may find certain ideas more useful than others, the book is designed with three learning alternatives, each meant to provide flexibility toward retaining and applying whatever is relevent to you:

1. There is an action heading and representative quote on each even-numbered page, to allow for quick reference and easy scanning.
2. There are detailed examples and illustrations on the odd-numbered pages, to allow for highlighting and more comprehensive support.
3. There are three keys included with each set of ideas, to allow for a summary of the major action points and for easy referral for planning.

There are *57 different keys* for increasing fees you will review by the time you finish this brief booklet. How many of these can apply to you? That's a matter of personal volition and intent. But remember this: If you improve just 1% a day, in 70 days you will be twice as good as you are at the outset. Are you currently improving at the rate of 1% a day? It sounds modest, but I've found that few people are.

I've provided 19 techniques and 57 keys for their successful application. Take your pick, or use them all. All you need is 1% a day to double your effectiveness in establishing professional fees which reflect your true value to your clients.

— Alan Weiss, Ph.D.

East Greenwich, RI

"When clients ask why
you cite a project fee
and not an hourly or
daily rate, illustrate
that it is for their own
protection."

THREE KEYS:
1. Value is in the eyes of the client.
2. Fees should be based upon fulfilling value, not performing tasks.
3. Time unit billing will always be less than your true value.

Fees should never be based on time units of any sort. If your value to a client is simply a matter of how many hours, days or weeks you provide, then you are no better than a commodity. Clients will understandably and rationally evaluate you as a commodity. Their legitimate questions will be "Can't you do it in less time?" "Do you need to take so many days?" and "What exactly is your hourly rate?"

Value must be based upon the worth which you bring to your client. The client's fee is an investment which bears a certain return. The return is in the eyes of the client, but you can help to manage that perception.

When clients ask why you cite a project fee and not an hourly or daily rate, illustrate that it is for their own protection. Only with an agreed-upon investment in return for an agreed-upon result can the client comfortably ask for extra time. Since there is no "meter running" there is no adverse consequence for the client to request an additional meeting, further review, more elaboration, etc. Reciprocally, there is no constraint upon you to request a further examination of certain areas, additional meetings, or more background, because there is no danger of being seen as attempting to increase "billable" units.

Just as I've never met an executive who complained that an "open door policy" was being abused by too many people walking through the door, I've never worked with a client who abused the option to request additional time within the scope of the project. However, it's vital that the project fee billing be clearly seen as a benefit to the client, as an alternative that saves money, and as an example of the trusting relationship which is being created.

There are a limited number of hours in the day. You usually cannot bill for more than eight hours in a normal working day, 40 hours in a normal working week. But there is no limit to the potential *value* which you bring to a client. How much is it worth to save a client money, to fend-off a legal problem, to improve morale, to enhance competitive edge, to provide peace of mind? I'll tell you how much—as much as the client values it. And that value will inevitably be more than several hours, or even several days, of your time.

"The difference between
the client's perception of
what is desired and your
ability to identify and
satisfy underlying need is
your value-added."

THREE KEYS:

1. Don't be concerned with today's business. Be concerned about building a long-term relationship.

2. Question whether what the client *says* is desired is really an effective resolution to underlying needs.

3. Enter into a collaborative quest to identify the cause of the "itch."

There is a fundamental difference between client "want" and client "need." All clients know what they want, but few can readily identify or articulate what they really need. The difference between the client's perception of what is desired and your ability to identify and satisfy underlying need is your value-added.

A client might want a will drawn-up because there is a need for estate planning. A client might ask for a training session on customer relations because there is too much attrition among existing accounts. A client might request a financial statement be prepared because there are refinancing opportunities which may be accessed.

Why do clients go to professionals for help? If it's simply to find someone to implement their own alternatives and wishes, then the professional provides very little value-added. The professional is only an implementor.

But if the professional can ask the questions—and establish the relationship—which allows underlying needs to be articulated, discussed and analyzed, the additional value is far beyond mere implementation. The professional is assisting in the client's strategy, whether personal or organizational. We are all satisfied when the computer repair people fix the application that keeps crashing. However, we are overjoyed when the service people suggest a program which fulfills our needs more quickly, at a better price, with greater scope, and/or in a more user-friendly fashion. Any client will pay more for being overjoyed than for being merely satisfied.

Never be satisfied yourself with merely fulfilling a request or completing a project. Find out what you can about why the client has the request (the "itch") that brought him or her to you. Don't worry about gaining a "sale," concern yourself with initiating a relationship from the earliest contact.

If you've cited a fee before finding out what has really brought the client to you, you are too concerned about your job and insufficiently concerned about your career. People will pay for the ability to assist in uncovering their own needs. To increase your value, you must be willing and able to engage in this quest.

"From that point on, you have joined the buyer in helping to negotiate your fee downward, and with the two of you working diligently together, the fee will spiral downward with surprising acceleration."

THREE KEYS

1. Never voluntarily offer options to reduce fees without being asked.

2. Do not reduce fees. Reduce value-added.

3. Never reduce a fee without a reduction in perceived value, or you are indicating that your fees are inflated and not value-based.

One of the most difficult objections we hear from a prospect is, "I'd love to use you, but we simply don't have the budget. It's not that we don't appreciate your value, it's just that we can't afford you." In all candor, how do you usually reply to this velvet rejection? If you're at all honest, most of you said, "Well, how much *can you afford?*"

From that point on, you have joined the buyer in helping to negotiate your fee downward, and with the two of you working diligently together, the fee will spiral downward with surprising acceleration. The weakness of professionals in replying to this objection is that they are focusing on the buyer's presumed budget for their activity, and not the buyer's overall budget in terms of value for the entire project.

Never negotiate fees. Negotiate value.

Every client will justifiably seek the best deal he or she can negotiate. However, there is an important dynamic to consider by the provider of the services sought: Clients, while eager to reduce fees, are loath to ever decrease value. Consequently, don't provide options to reduce your fee unless you are providing commensurate examples of the value which will be removed from the project.

A CPA preparing tax returns might "remove" the year-to-year comparisons which enable the taxpayer to easily evaluate successful tax strategies. A consultant might "remove" written reports or personal presentations of a study's results. A financial planner might "remove" the quarterly newsletter providing important changes to IRA requirements. An attorney might "remove" an offer of telephone consultation at reduced fees on workman's compensation cases.

Some of my colleagues immediately tell clients that there are options to lower the fee without the client even inquiring! My reaction is to say, "Of course fees can be negotiated. What value would you like to remove from the project?"

Once you are known as someone who will reduce fees without a *quid pro quo*, you will be expected to do so every time. It is better to allow business to walk away than to become known as someone who readily reduces fees under pressure.

"The problem, of course, is that the prospect can say either 'yes' or 'no.' I have never liked those odds."

THREE KEYS:

1. Only you can provide the choice of yeses. Do it every time.

2. Don't allow the prospect to make a simple "yes or no" decision.

3. Provide at least one choice which is large and comprehensive, because clients don't like to pass-up value.

One of the worst traits of professional services firms is their determination to provide an alternative for the client to "buy." Even the best of listeners and most expert of those who can identify needs often delimit their income by establishing *the* alternative. The problem, of course, is that the prospect can say either "yes" or "no." I have never liked those odds.

The ideal approach is to provide the prospect with a "choice of yeses." Instead of the prospect trying to determine whether or not to use your services, the prospect is in a position to try to determine *which of your options to choose.* The most notable dynamic about this approach is that it is controlled by you, not the buyer.

While the prospect may still say "no" to your range of alternatives (the choice of yeses), the odds are greatly reduced. In fact, the prospect might supply an alternative in addition to yours, or might ask that two or more be combined. In these cases the prospect is assisting in closing the sale.

The choice of yeses should not be simply more of your basic service, provided over a longer time frame. The choice should clearly portray differences in value for different investments. A financial planner might offer basic tax planning, tax planning plus estate planning, tax planning plus estate planning plus investment advice for children, or all of the above plus access at any time on an 800 number to respond to client concerns and questions. Each of these requires a different level of investment. Let the client decide how much value is needed in return for how much investment. (Don't be afraid to make one choice a large, comprehensive relationship. Remember, clients hate to negotiate away value.)

Always explain to prospects what their "range of options" is, and include those options which you've identified as *not* being viable choices, to show the prospect that you have carefully considered what is feasible and what is not. This kind of alternative generation is a relatively simple undertaking, but it represents tremendous initial value in the eyes of the client.

"By beginning with client objectives, you are performing an essential service to the client, who might not have clarified his or her objectives..."

THREE KEYS:

1. Early in the conversation, always ask the QGTRIHF.

2. Broaden objectives to arrive at true underlying need.

3. Structure your response to fulfill the need, providing a choice of yeses.

There is a question guaranteed to result in higher fees (QGTRIHF). It's a simple question, but one that is infrequently asked, because the professional is too concerned about acquiring the quick dollar. However, once asked, the prospect will actively help the professional to seek out needs and respond to them.

Unlike the downward spiral that occurs when both buyer and seller collaborate to lower fees because of "insufficient budget," the QGTRIHF creates an updraft which lifts the conversation, the scope and the value of what you will deliver. The QGTRIHF is:

What Are Your Objectives?

Think about the conversations you have with prospects and clients. Most often they involve *presumed* objectives, against which you are providing alternatives (or, worse, the prospect has already selected alternatives and you are asked merely to implement). It's a very small endeavor, and of little differentiated value, to purchase a security or to deliver a training program or to list a house for sale. Those are all pre-determined alternatives selected by the client. It is somewhat broader and more differentiated to counsel on the range of securities available, design a training program, and suggest what investment should be made in the house to enhance the sale price.

But the greatest differentiation—and, therefore, the greatest value-added—is in creating an overall financial planning approach, designing a human resources development strategy, and positioning the house in select, diverse media to draw high-potential purchasers. These three gradations in each of the examples are possible outcomes of identical prospect interactions. The most value and largest potential business (scope of project, long-term involvement, size of sale, etc.) are a question of asking the prospect "What are your objectives?" prior to engaging in alternatives, brain-storming, planning or, heaven forfend, citing fees.

By beginning with client objectives, you are performing an essential service to the client, who might not have clarified his or her objectives, and who might be considering inappropriate responses. (A training program will not reduce turnover if the cause of the turnover is superior competitive products. Improving the interior of a house will not result in a higher purchase price if qualified buyers aren't found. A contemporary investment may be inappropriate for someone carrying excessive credit line indebtedness.)

When you sit down with a prospect, *what are your objectives?*

Don't Sit by the Phone. Use It.

> "Ensure that clients *and* prospects are aware of *all* of your services."

THREE KEYS:

1. Ensure that clients *and* prospects are aware of *all* of your services.

2. Search for innovative ways to remain in front of buyers.

3. Don't be bashful about pursuing existing clients.

Many professionals I've observed and counseled have been intent on giving services and value away for free. I have no objection to such humanitarian ends, but if you're in business to make money and pay the mortgage, I have reservations about such a strategy.

Just as people new in a business often have the misguided notion that the public will beat down the door, veteran professionals often labor under the misconception that the prospect is magically aware of all the services which are available. If raising fees is directly correlated to raising perceived value, then it naturally follows that the prospect should be apprised of the available value at every convenient opportunity.

For prospects, it is incumbent upon you to allow the full breadth of your products and services to be communicated. Printed material—such as brochures, newsletters, articles, advertising, interviews—is ideal for this purpose, so long as it is continually in circulation. Prospects do not generally keep files labeled "some day I might need this person." More often, they select a service professional at the time they feel the "itch." Consequently, it's important that you are visible in some fashion on a regular basis, since you have no way of predicting the timing of the itch.

Public speaking and civic participation are also important, inexpensive methods to reach prospects with both your abilities and public-mindedness. Speaking at service club functions, at the chamber of commerce and at local school events are ideal alternatives. Serving on non-profit boards and volunteering for fund-raising activities and charity work are others. You will literally be rubbing elbows with prospects and recommenders. Corporate officers often belong to and volunteer for these same functions, and individual buyers abound.

For existing clients, too many professionals make the assumption that they will call when they need something. Remember, clients don't always know what they need, and you don't always know who's been industriously trying to gain their attention while you're waiting for the phone to ring. Personal touches such as holiday greetings, birthday or anniversary remembrances, contributions to a charity in the name of your clients, personal notes, clippings of interest from relevant publications, and a personal client newsletter are excellent methods to remain a reliable and trusted advisor and friend.

How many of these activities do you engage in on a regular basis? Are you sitting by the phone, or are you using it? Are you reading the paper, or are you writing for it? Are you listening to dull speeches, or delivering energetic ones?

Tie Fees to Areas of Greatest Value

"Are you a financial planner with distinct services (you visit the client's home), a consultant with breakthrough relationships (you provide a 24-hour personal number to CEOs)..."

THREE KEYS:

1. Recognize that you cannot be breakthrough in all elements.
2. Identify where you can provide the maximum value-added.
3. Always consider the client's perspective of worth, not your own.

One of the essential elements in establishing high fees is to create a proactive strategic profile for your marketplace. Your profile involves three elements: your products, your services, and your relationships. In any of these three areas you may choose to be competitive (as good as the next person), distinct (seen to have some distinguishing features), or break-through (the absolute leading edge in the field). Whatever the choice, the determination must be yours, and not forged by your competition, the economy or the way you feel on any given day.

	Competitve	Distinct	Breakthrough
Product			
Service			
Relationship			

There is not an intrinsic advantage to being "breakthrough" in every category. It might be too expensive, or impractical, or unnecessary. However, you must *proactively* decide how you will appear to the public.

Your fee structure should be tied to the areas of greatest value delivery, and that will determine how you invest your money, how you spend your time, what kind of people you hire or collaborate with, the nature of your publicity, etc. Is your true value in your product (a manual, a contract, a guide), your service (morale increased, money saved, confidence restored) or your relationships (trust, accessibility, guidance, etc.)? In many cases, professionals watch what the competition is doing and try to emulate it. The weakness of such an approach is that you are playing according to someone else's rules, on their field, and with their ball.

Establish your own strategy, your own "turf," and your own profile. Are you a financial planner with distinct services (you visit the client's home), a consultant with breakthrough relationships (you provide a 24-hour personal number to CEOs), an attorney with competitive products (standard wills and contracts), a realtor with breakthrough service (you will, for an extra fee, arrange for house-sitting, school interviews, etc.)? Determine how your strategic profile best guarantees obvious, perceived value to the client.

"If you cannot obtain
conceptual agreement,
fees are academic,
because you're not able
to assist the prospect
and form a helping
client relationship."

THREE KEYS:

1. Send a proposal as a confirmation, not an exploration.

2. Base all proposals on absolute conceptual agreement.

3. Don't feel obligated to cite fees prior to sending the proposal.

When providing a proposal for a prospect or client, you should expect at least a 60% acceptance rate. (I average slightly over 80%.) The entire nature of proposals is often mistaken by the creators. Proposals should not be a sailing expedition to see if the prospect will agree on a course. They should be the final line tying the boat securely to the dock.

Whether offering an individualized plan of action to an investor or a comprehensive contract to a major organization, proposals should reflect the conceptual agreement already concluded. If no conceptual agreement has been concluded, then how do you know what to include in the proposal, how to deliver it, and what to charge for its worth?

Conceptual agreement means reaching common acknowledgment of the client's needs, objectives to be met, options to meet them, measurement criteria, follow-up, and both parties' accountabilities. Adjust these as you will for your business, but if the client recognizes a comfortable plan of action with excellent value, *the fee will seldom be an issue.* Most prospects will, understandably, want to discuss fees early. Too early. Unfortunately, many professionals allow that discussion to take place prematurely.

When a prospect inquires about fees, it is not only reasonable but also professionally responsible to reply, "I'll be happy to detail the fees once I understand how I might be able to help you. First, I'd like to hear about your objectives…" If you discuss fees—even a range of fees—early in the conversation, the prospect will be focusing on how to reduce them. If you focus on objectives to be met, the prospect will focus on *how to maximize them.*

Once there is conceptual agreement, place the entire conversation in an orderly format in your proposal, and include your fee for the entire range of services (always offering the choice of yeses, with appropriate fees). If you cannot obtain conceptual agreement, fees are academic, because you're not able to assist the prospect and form a helping client relationship. Conceptual agreement isn't merely a matter of effective fee-setting, it is integral to a successful, long-term client relationship.

Sending proposals "blindly" through the mail or providing them without conceptual agreement about what is to be achieved is like turning on the hose and hoping that your car gets washed. It might happen, but don't bet on it.

"...if you lower fees with no reason *apparent to the customer*, there is only one inescapable conclusion that the customer can draw..."

THREE KEYS:

1. Never offer to unilaterally reduce your fee.

2. Do offer *quid pro quo* options of value to reduce fees for benefits.

3. Let overly-demanding and troublesome business walk out the door.

Never provide a discounted fee without a *quid pro quo*. Consultants and speakers are forever providing opportunities for their clients to pay them less money. One standard example is this statement found in many letters and proposals: "Mary Jones usually charges $2,500 per day, but is pleased to offer her services on this project for $1,750 per day." Or this: "Our normal commission rate is 7%, but we can reduce that to 6% as a gesture of good will." Why?

There are valid reasons for offering reduced fees even though value doesn't decline. One is advance payment. For the use of the money and elimination of the need to bill, financial consideration makes sense. Another is multiple bookings, when the volume justifies lower fees in return for the guaranteed future business. A third is referrals *which lead to business*, since your client has helped to generate revenue.

However, if you lower fees with no reason *apparent to the customer*, there is only one inescapable conclusion that the customer can draw:

> ## "These fees can be lowered still further if I find the right leverage!"

Usually that leverage is the threat to delay, to do business elsewhere, to "shop around," to ask cousin Louie, to do anything that vaguely threatens the tenuous relationship that exists. And these tactics usually work in the buyer's favor.

Such leverage isn't nearly as powerful if the service professional doesn't open that particular door to begin with. "Sorry, I don't lower my fees, unless there is some value I'm providing that we can remove. However, we can discuss options for you to take action to reduce them. For example, we offer a single-payment discount..." If a prospect taps at the door to lower fees and it swings open, the prospect will waltz in. That's what happens when you offer to lower fees. But if the client pushes on the door and it doesn't budge, the client will probably not choose to try to knock it down. That's what happens when you are resolute about what you are worth.

The amazing fact is that most professionals manage to lower their own fees without much more than a gentle touch by the prospect. It's like folding a poker hand of four kings because the other player states, "Well, I finally drew that royal flush. I hope no one is foolish enough to stay in the game!"

Don't fold your hand. In our business, it costs nothing to see all of the cards.

"Technology and delivery are often assumed to be one activity. They are not."

THREE KEYS:

1. Always use an objective fee apportionment when collaborating or contracting.

2. Sharing fees does not mean lowering compensation for your value.

3. Any collaborator must provide their own tangible value-added.

I f you must share fees with another party in a collaborative effort, apportion them based upon objective contribution, period. I have found it simple to partition any sales into three elements: acquisition, technology, and delivery. You may have additional elements, but there aren't too many others.

The *acquisition* is traditionally called the "close." Someone must be responsible for getting the buyer—whether corporate officer, family, individual, purchasing agent, executor or anyone else—to sign a check. The *technology* is represented by the content of the intervention required. If you are selling a seminar, there is an instructional technology. If you are creating a trust, there is a financial planning technology. There is always a transfer of skills, provision of expertise (i.e., appraising a stamp collection), or tangible product provided. The *delivery* is the process of the intervention—training a group, drawing up a document, assessing a vintage automobile. Note that I might deliver—assess the automobile—using someone else's technology—a set of criteria and checklists I apply to place a value on the vehicle.

Technology and delivery are often assumed to be one activity. They are not.

If you accept my three elements, it's simple to divide the total engagement

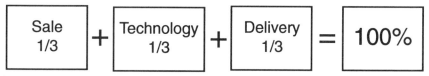

into thirds. In a $30,000 sale, if I acquire and deliver it using your technology, I would deserve $20,000 and you would deserve $10,000. In the same situation, if you and I divided the delivery equally, then I would receive $15,000 ($10,000 for the sale and $5,000 for the delivery) as would you ($10,000 for the technology and $5,000 for the delivery).

The full amount of the contract must reflect what you and I feel is fair for our respective roles. If I'm working for five days in delivery and receiving only $5,000, I may feel that we are under-evaluating my worth. The basic premise is that the distribution isn't based upon time, but upon contribution to overall success. The technology ownership does not require time, but represents significant value-added which should be compensated.

Many professionals who contract with others to deliver business for them overlook the value of their own expertise, technology and products. Consequently, they overpay the contractee while underpaying themselves. (Note that you may change the apportionment if you feel the three elements are uneven, i.e., pay 50% for acquisition, 25% for technology and 25% for delivery, or any variation thereof.)

"One of the wonderful aspects of personal services firms is that you can provide a wide array of value. Some of that value lies in enabling the client to deal with one person instead of many."

THREE KEYS:

1 Seek to laterally increase fees through assistance in additional areas.

2. Don't be bound by current competence—build or acquire more.

3. Escape time/unit billing by providing value in non-traditional areas.

One excellent method to increase fees is by earning fees that would have gone to others. One of the wonderful aspects of personal services firms is that you can provide a wide array of value. Some of that value lies in enabling the client to deal with one person instead of many.

Personal services are based upon trust. However, it's a difficult and often time-consuming process for a client to find and utilize a professional whom he or she trusts. Many clients find out the hard way, having to abandon someone referred to them because the relationship simply doesn't work. We've all seen houses for sale which seem to change listing agencies at the end of each contract like clockwork, people who have their taxes completed by a different CPA each year (or attempt to do even complex returns themselves), and organizations which are simultaneously using five different consulting firms.

The tremendous advantage for the professional in investing in relationship building isn't merely the repeat business; it's the *additional* business. Clients who may say "I don't have the budget" really mean that they don't have the budget for higher fees for services already being considered or performed by you. But they usually have budget for other services which could be performed by you.

It's not unusual for a speaker to also serve as a panelist or panel moderator; for a financial planner to also serve as tax preparer or trust executor; for an attorney to also serve on the client's board of directors; for a realtor to provide placement services for the "trailing spouse"; or for an architect do offer landscaping design as well as house design. A friend of mine who is an attorney specializing in dental practices found himself engaged more and more in brokering the financing and sale of those practices. I helped him to establish a consulting approach which undertakes that work irrespective of any legal requirements. Last year his consulting work far outpaced his legal work, and his overall income was almost 500% of his best year as an attorney. (And not incidentally, this increase is also attributable to his escape from the hour billing system of the legal profession. As a consultant, he bills based upon value of his services or a percent of the financing.)

Professional relationships are built on trust. Once the trust is established, you may move laterally to other areas of client assistance that are within your competence (or competence you are able to acquire). This is why the big accounting firms all launched consulting divisions. Once the client trusts you with the money, it's not difficult to trust you with management advice. Today, Arthur Andersen is the largest consulting firm in the world.

"When should you reduce your fee? Only to gain future value or larger shares of business."

THREE KEYS:

1. Reducing or eliminating fees should be an infrequent action.

2. Short-term sacrifices should be made only for clear long-term gains.

3. Fee changes are solely your decision, never the client's.

There are some occasions when you may intelligently decide to reduce fees in return for higher fees at a later point. However, these opportunities are rare, and are often used as a rationalization to take business at any cost. Architects, in particular, seem vulnerable to this trap, because they see themselves "completing projects" and not running a business. I've known architects who will take a loss on a project because they so badly want to design the building. When I ask how they will compensate for the loss, they inevitably respond, "volume."

First, let's clarify the times when you should *never* accept work at a lower fee than you have cited:

• The client asks you to do so because there "is no budget."

• The competition is citing a lower fee (and, presumably, lower value).

• You don't want to lose the business.

In these instances, in best case you will still lose the business, and in worst case you *will get* the business at a fee which doesn't provide proper remuneration for your value, and which you will be "locked into" in all future dealings *as the starting point from which the client will demand that you decrease fees still further.*

When should you reduce your fee? Only to gain future value or larger shares of business. Here are the obvious cases:

• The client knows that you are providing a non-traditional service for the first time and, in return for the client serving as "laboratory," you will accept a one-time lower fee. (Example: A financial services consultant is delivering a seminar on understanding balance sheets to management personnel.)

• You are subcontracting for someone else behind the scenes, and bear no marketing expense nor overhead for the business. (Example: An attorney has asked a realtor to review some non-standard contracts and provide an opinion on their propriety.)

• A good, long-standing client in a temporary predicament asks a favor. (Example: A contractor suffering a horrible quarter in terms of cash flow asks an attorney who has handled all prior work to review a minor contractual change. The attorney shouldn't defer payment, but should waive it.)

• There is legitimate justification for *pro bono* work in a charity, state agency, educational institution, non-profit association, etc. (Example: The organization combating drug addiction needs help in strategic planning, auditing, renovations, etc.) Remember, *pro bono* work is a conscious choice and investment, it is not business for which you tried to get a fee but couldn't!

"Higher fees often imply
higher competence and
better service in the
eyes of the buyer..."

THREE KEYS:

1. Determine a consistent position for fees within the market ranges.

2. If you don't know the market ranges, you're probably *under*charging.

3. Remember that higher fees tend to influence buyers as "higher value."

P ositioning strategies are helpful if you intend to occupy a particular market niche. For example, you might be a "boutique" business, not as large as the nationally-known monoliths, but more substantive than the moonlighting college professor. Or you just may *be* the moonlighting professor who is able to offer high credibility with zero overhead costs.

The best way to establish fees with this strategy is to determine the array of services you are providing (which may be only one, but if you've read this far, should be many more!), determine what the range of fees is for each service in

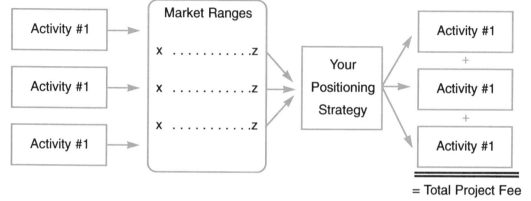

the marketplace, identify where you want to be in that range (high, middle, low), and build a project fee accordingly. You may seek to be in the high end of a range for one service and the low end of a range for a different service. However, it's more common to be in a fairly consistent range for all services, since the client isn't able to identify such fine distinctions within a total project fee. *There is nothing wrong with deliberately seeking to be in the lower range of the market as a strategic decision.*

For example, many professional speakers who could easily charge higher fees choose to deliberately remain in lower ranges in order to maximize the volume of their work, and to be seen as accessible to wider groups and organizations. Usually, the decision to be in the higher end of the range will also require a commensurate investment in image and profile, since perception is reality for many buyers.

Finally, and most importantly in deciding on positioning with fee ranges, most buyers expect to get what they pay for. Higher fees often imply higher competence and better service in the eyes of the buyer, and the buyer actually adjusts evaluation of performance based upon their association of high quality with high fees!

Assess Your Contribution to the Outcome

"Here are the
questions you can first
ask yourself, and then
ask the client, to assist
in determining your
contribution to the
business or personal
goals of the organiza-
tion or individual."

THREE KEYS:

1. The client and you must agree on the worth you provide at the outset.

2. Value includes qualitative as well as quantitative considerations.

3. This assessment should be managed by you and serve as a template to gauge success during the relationship.

ow do you determine your value to the client? Is it a "gut feel" which varies, depending on the day, the mood or the bank account? Or are there methods with which you can determine your worth to the client, above and beyond days spent or activities completed?

Here are the questions you can first ask yourself, and then ask the client, to assist in determining your contribution to the business or personal goals of the organization or individual. They can easily be amended for any type of personal services profession.

- What is the outcome of this effort worth?
    - If quantitative, what is the amount?
    - If qualitative, what are the effects?
    - How does the client describe a successful outcome?
    - To what degree is the client's condition improved?
- What is your *direct* contribution to the outcome?
    - Are you accelerating what is already occurring?
    - Is the outcome dependent upon your unique talents?
    - Are you facilitating actively and often?
    - Are you observing, diagnosing, and/or prescribing?
- What is the current relationship with the client?
    - Is this a long-time client?
    - Are you gaining in professional growth?
    - Does the assignment present stressful conditions?
    - Are there difficult and inflexible deadlines?
- What are your costs in completing this assignment?
    - Were there marketing and other acquisition costs?
    - Are additional staff and sub-contractors required?
    - Are there extensive travel requirements?
    - Are there elaborate materials and deliverables required?

You might seek to add additional questions, but if you can answer these satisfactorily with the client's concurrence, you can establish a very accurate quantitative assessment of your worth. If you can't readily answer these questions, then you have more work to do in establishing conceptual agreement.

"Consequently, unless you provide increased value to existing clients, pressure on fees will always be downward. And unless you are willing to charge higher fees for new clients joining you, there will be no relief on that end, either."

THREE KEYS:

1. Introduce new value to existing clients in order to raise fees.

2. Do not accept referral business on the same basis as the referent.

3. Maximize perceived value and fees in all new business sales.

F ees should be different for new clients as compared to those of existing clients. There is nothing unethical or impractical about this strategy. In fact, one can make a strong case that long-term clients deserve the benefits of your familiarity with their circumstances. And there is no surer way to destroy a relationship than for long-term clients to discover that they are paying higher fees than new clients for similar services.

Make no mistakes about this philosophy: It is extraordinarily difficult to raise fees for the same services within existing client accounts. When my financial advisors raised their fees for corporate and personal tax returns one year, I asked them how that could possibly have happened, since the complexity of the returns had not changed. They responded that overhead was increasing. I replied that they should be offsetting that by spending fewer hours on my work, since they were very familiar with it, and by the fact that I had hired a bookkeeper at their urging, whose very job should be reducing their work. After all, why should I pay the bookkeeper to perform work their firm was doing, if they are going to charge me the same fees anyway?

My financial advisors adjusted my fee downward, and haven't raised it since. I admire their protection of our relationship, but I bemoan their strategy for fee-setting. They should be bringing on new clients at higher rates (not just more hours spent), and seeking to reduce rates for established clients. However, they should be also striving to provide established clients with *new* products and services, for which additional value is perceived, allowing for additional fees.

Once a client is able to discern a rate structure—which is why billable time units are anathema—value doesn't count. And the client will justifiably seek to reduce the factors which drive up the rate structure. Consequently, unless you provide increased value to existing clients, pressure on fees will always be downward. And unless you are willing to charge higher fees for new clients joining you, there will be no relief on that end, either.

If you use clearly-discernible rate structures, referral business (the very lifeblood of professional services firms) will already know the rates charged to established clients, and will expect the same. If you use value-based fees, existing clients can't readily cite a structure and new clients will have to elaborate their objectives, allowing you to set fees based on the fulfillment of need.

Never increase fees in existing clients unless you change the value you are providing. Always seek to maximize fees with new clients, since they should subsidize your development of such additional value for all clients.

Fearlessly Raise Fees for Difficult Business

"The client demands
delayed billing,
contingency billing or
any other special
payment terms..."

THREE KEYS:

1. Recognize that some business is acceptable only at a premium fee.
2. Be mentally prepared to walk away from difficult business, which will help you demand the appropriate fee structure.
3. Raise fees until your level of discomfort is alleviated.

There are times when you should fearlessly raise fees because you are quite content to walk away from the business. The business is within your competence, and you can provide genuine value to the client, but there are conditions and circumstances which make the engagement somewhat unattractive. Assuming that you would not reject the work out-of-hand (i.e., it requires too much time away from home, conflicts with your belief system, would endanger other client relationships) but wouldn't be crushed if you lost it, you may readily increase fees in these instances:

- There is significant travel required.

- You would have to invest significant time learning the client's business or understanding highly technical issues.

- Large amounts of time on tedious details are required.

- Significant sub-contracting is necessary for completion.

- Large amounts of custom-designed materials are requested.

- The client will own the copyright to materials produced.

- You must acquire or rent specific equipment or instruments.

- You name cannot be associated with the project.

- You must work for and accommodate several different decision makers with differing interests.

- You must cooperate with and coordinate the work of other professionals over whom you do not possess actual authority.

- The client demands delayed billing, contingency billing or any other special payment terms.

- The client has previously been difficult to work with.

- The nature of the assignment involves work sensitive to litigation, malpractice and/or conflict.

- The buyer is requesting that you perform work which is acknowledged to be unpopular with the employees and/or implementors.

- Competitors of yours have experienced difficulties with this client.

- The value-added you are providing is highly qualitative and difficult to measure objectively.

- There is a danger that the buyer will change during the course of the engagement.

Difficult business is not necessarily poor business, *provided you have taken action to ensure that you are compensated for your discomfort, hard work and expense.*

"The key indicator for business which should be 'abandoned' is any fee which is more than 15% below the average for the firm's business..."

THREE KEYS:

1. Regularly examine your client base to cull low-end business.

2. You are not obligated to retain clients, but you are obligated to ensure that they are properly treated while retained.

3. You cannot reach out without letting go.

A bandon the bottom 10% of your business base at least every other year. That sounds harsh, but you are actually doing a favor for both your clients and your bank account, because most professional service firms have clients "hanging around" who aren't being served well.

In a misguided belief that "all business is good business," many professionals continue to serve (and even seek) clients which were appropriate at a very different stage of the firm's growth. Interior designers may start by doing small window treatments; consultants by providing individual hiring interviews; realtors by listing very inexpensive homes; CPAs by preparing low-income tax returns; attorneys by doing home closings. At the time, all of these activities made sense because they made cents. However, as the firm has grown, these activities provide only marginal profit and consume disproportionate amounts of time, communication and energy.

Conversely, these long-time clients or activities are almost always poorly-served. They take a lower priority to higher-profit, higher-profile work, and are "expendable" in terms of deadlines and commitments. The solution to these emotional but not intelligent attachments is to formally review status at least every two years. Larger firms should do this annually.

The key indicator for business which should be "abandoned" is any fee which is more than 15% below the average for the firm's business (not for *similar* business, because that merely encourages the continuation of those bottom-rung clients). Such business should be referred to other professionals who are in a better position to effectively handle it. In some cases, this could be junior people in your operation, but usually it means people in the position you were in when you first took on the business. Both the client and your firm will be better served by treating these clients realistically.

Through this disciplined "culling" of the client base, you free-up the time and resources to pursue and service clients at the top-end of your fee structure. You cannot reach out to higher levels without letting go of the lower levels. You only have two arms. Finally, don't attempt to secure a referral fee or commission when referring such clients elsewhere. The small amounts involved will only increase the client's overall cost and still won't be worth the attention you'll have to provide, since you would still be ethically and pragmatically bound to the account. The firms to which they are referred might well reciprocate with business more appropriate for you. Let go, and reach out.

"The old sales aphorism is that you never get a sale you don't ask for. In many cases, simply stating that 'our terms are payment in full at time of agreement,' will generate a check without further discussion."

THREE KEYS:

1. Ask for payment terms most beneficial to you every time.

2. Offer incentives for early payment if you must.

3. Never accept payment subject to conditions upon completion.

T he value of fees can often be maximized without ever raising the level of fees themselves. That's because *control of the velocity of the fee* can be as important as the actual amount. To say it another way, money in your bank account is worth infinitely more than money promised you but not received.

The absolute best way to collect fees and maximize their velocity is to get paid in full, in advance. Impossible, you say? Eighty percent of my clients pay in full, in advance. (And how do *you* pay for purchases made by credit card, whether in person, by mail order, or by phone?) There are two methods to use to accomplish payment in advance (or, technically, at the time of agreement for your services):

1. Ask for it.

2. Provide an incentive.

The old sales aphorism is that you never get a sale you don't ask for. In many cases, simply stating that "our terms are payment in full at time of agreement," will generate a check without further discussion. Most service professionals never ask.

If the direct request will not work, try offering a mild incentive. "Our terms are 50% payable at agreement, and 50% in 45 days. However, you may avail yourself of a 10% reduction in the fee by paying the entire amount upon agreement." Many people see such an incentive as too good to pass up. And if you've reached conceptual agreement, and the client trusts you, the deal looks even better. Why should you sacrifice 10% simply to obtain payment early? Again, there are two reasons:

1. You have use of the money, no billing to worry about, no possibility of an overdue receivable, a better profile with your banker, and full client commitment.

2. The client will not tend to cancel the agreement. (You could have a non-cancellation clause, but this sometimes deters people from paying in advance.)

If you cannot get payment in advance, seek at least 50% (if you're billing by time units, this is extraordinarily difficult, which is why that method is so poor). The worst way to be remunerated is by non-contractual, periodic retainer, and the thing you should virtually never do unless the deal is exceptional is to accept contingency fees (contingency fee attorneys, excepted). Full fee upon completion, or full fee subject to certain conditions being met are sure ways to enable clients to change their minds, find fault, delay payment, or simply not pay because their own financial conditions have deteriorated in the interim.

"As a professional engaged in providing service to your clients, the immediate urge may be to 'fix' what ails the client. However, the long-term goals are best met by *improving the client's condition.*"

THREE KEYS:

1. Focus on improvement, not merely "fixing."

2. Approach clients with proactive ideas; don't wait for their problems.

3. Charge higher fees for improvement than you do for "fixes."

Maximize your value-added to clients by helping them to achieve higher levels of performance, return, quality and comfort. Although most clients have problems they want solved, don't view yourself as merely a problem solver. "Fixing" things will simply restore the prior performance or condition, which is comfortable, but limits value. However, if you improve their condition—innovate—you'll provide limitless value for clients.

If a client has a problem with the IRS on a tax return, why not also provide help in preventing similar inquiries in the future? If a client wants to renovate a recreation area, why not suggest how it could be turned into a home entertainment center? If a client requires an employee survey, why not recommend that the customers participate? As a professional engaged in providing service to your clients, the immediate urge may be to "fix" what ails the client. However, the long-term goals are best met by *improving the client's condition*. It seldom makes more sense to place a bucket under a leak than it does to fix the roof, and a patched roof is seldom as good as a new one. What are you offering in the way of long-term improvement?

Problem Solving

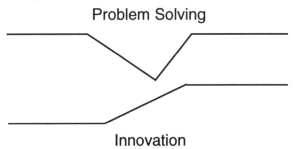

Innovation

In the graphic above, the top progression represents problem solving: Something is working well, it declines, you recognize it, and you fix it. Conditions are restored to their prior level. The bottom progression is innovation: Something is working well, and you help to make it even better. The former is reactive, and in response to a problem. The latter is proactive and in anticipation of improvement. Most people readily feel the former (there's a complaint, money lost, time wasted, etc.). But most do not recognize the value of the latter. In helping clients to proactively improve in anticipation of future conditions, you are providing unique and high-value assistance.

We stated earlier that clients usually know what they want. Often, that's a result of being in a "fix it" mentality. However, we pointed out that clients seldom appreciate what they need, which is a key avenue for the professional to provide value-added assistance. Identifying opportunity and innovation is the fast lane on that avenue.

"You can't help your clients if you aren't helping yourself."

THREE KEYS:

1. _____

2 _____

3. _____

There is nothing intrinsically unethical, illogical, impractical or illegal about trying to maximize the fees you charge your clients. If you raise fees beyond the value that clients perceive in the relationship, market forces will drive them away. Conversely, if they perceive even more value for your services than you are charging, there will be no reciprocal pressure from the market to drive fees up. You must control this dynamic, or you will chronically suffer from the lack of control.

The traditional advice to professionals has been to "raise fees when demand exceeds supply." That's plain silly. For one thing, demand may never exceed supply. After all, you have 365 days in a year, 24 hours a day—you can squeeze a lot of supply in there. For another, who says you have to be fully booked and constantly working to demand premium income? Working hard and working smart have never been synonymous.

Why do some attorneys justify higher fees than others for equivalent work? Why are some financial advisors worth more, even though they may spend fewer hours with a client? Why do some speakers earn five times what others do for a keynote address? Why do some realtors receive calls requesting to have houses listed while others have to make cold calls and walk the streets to pick up even a few?

The answer is in the value perceived by the client. What are you doing each day to improve the perceived value for current clients and prospective clients? What are you doing to build relationships and public profile? What are you doing to broaden your skills and increase your access to additional resources? If the answer to those questions is "not much," the market will take care of you. That is, you will stagnate. If the answer is, "every day I'm making improvements, taking risks, and growing," then you will be controlling your market. You can't help your clients if you aren't helping yourself.

What have you gained from reading this booklet, and how will you apply the ideas? Thus far, you've been passive. Now it's time to be innovative and proactive. The final three keys are yours. What will you do—immediately—to begin to maximize the value you are providing clients and the fees you are charging? Every day you delay, you are losing money, less able to enjoy your success and, ironically, less able to help your clients. What are you going to do about it? Choose any of the ideas and approaches in this book, modify them for your professional practice, and list specifically what you intend to do:

Now Do It!

There are additional resources to help you listed on the following pages.

Books

Million Dollar Consulting: The Professional's Guide to Growing A Practice
McGraw-Hill: 1992, 1994 (274 pages, soft cover)

The definitive work on dramatically growing a consulting business. For the single practitioner, small firm principal, or aspiring consultant. The section on fee-setting alone is worth the price of the book. Main selection of the Fortune and Business Week Book Clubs. "If you're interested in becoming a rich consultant, this book is a must read." —Robert F. Mager, Founder and President, Mager Associates, member, Training & Development Hall of Fame.

Best Laid Plans: Turning Strategy Into Action Throughout Your Organization
HarperCollins: 1990; Las Brisas Research Press: 1994 (254 pages, hard cover)

How to implement strategy for any size organization, public or private, based upon the author's actual strategy work. Most strategy does not fail in its formulation, it fails in its implementation. This book addresses that failing. "I would have helped The New York Times company more if I had read it ten years ago."—Jack Harrison, Pulitzer Prize-winning Group President.

Managing for Peak Performance: A Guide to the Power (and Pitfalls) of Personal Style
HarperCollins: 1989; Las Brisas Research Press: 1994 (177 pages, hard cover)

Techniques for understanding and influencing others, including self-tests, instruments, guidelines and checklists for assessing style. Translated into German. Useful for stress reduction, selection, decision making and negotiating. "A uniquely practical set of guidelines for managing to get the results you need."—P. Roy Vagelos, Chairman and CEO, Merck & Co., Inc.

The Innovation Formula: How Organizations Turn Change Into Opportunity
(with Michel Robert) HarperCollins: 1988, 1990 (126 pages, soft cover)

The classic book on the process of innovation, for the individual as well as the organization. Translated into German and Italian. Provides tangible, measurable means to identify, evaluate and implement innovative ideas, including the assessment of risk. "A rational, sensible approach to making innovation a repeatable process."—Robert D. Kennedy, CEO, Union Carbide.

Cassettes

Peak Performance: Mastering Change, Why Winners Win, Million Dollar Consulting
Infomedix: 1993 (three tapes, running time 195 minutes)

Live keynote speeches before international management audiences, describing how to leverage one's talent and keep focused on the goal. Useful for professional and personal pursuits, with techniques that can be applied immediately. "Hard-hitting, no-nonsense— Alan simply wows 'em."—Dr. William Winter, President, American Press Institute.

Ordering information on page 51.

ADDITIONAL RESOURCES FOR PROFESSIONALS FROM ALAN WEISS

Booklets: The Professional Development Series from Las Brisas Research Press

How to Maximize Fees in Professional Service Firms: A Handbook for Professionals in Consulting, Law, Finance, Architecture, Real Estate and Other Services

The methods for creating high-value client relationships and receiving commensurate fees for that value. Provides a provocative set of questions, keys and approaches which any professional can apply to his or her practice, irrespective of the field. Useful for the individual practitioner, small business owner, or individual member of any professional services firm.

Rejoicing in Diversity: How to Accept and Embrace Diversity for its Intrinsic Value

The antithesis of "managing diversity," this work enables managers to understand the *value* of diversity in terms of pragmatic business goals. Deals with the subtle and mis-understood barriers, and provides techniques to create an organization richer for its diverse nature. Equally useful as a guide for line management and as a basis for human resource professionals to build educational programs.

Doing Well by Doing Right: Guidelines for Ethical Management Practices

Why ethical management is a practical business requirement, and how to identify and eliminate ethical dilemmas. Provides insight into internal conflicts and customer con-flicts, and the surprising reasons for most unethical behavior on the job. Effective for individual learning and for workshops utilizing group discussion.

Raising the Bar Every Day: Continuous Improvement As A Way of Life

How to anticipate, recognize and exploit opportunity, whether on the job or in one's personal life. Provides examples from the public and private sectors, on the small and grand scale, as to how opportunity is always knocking but few recognize the sound. Includes sources of opportunity, how to escape problem solving, and how to reward the process.

Leadership Every Day: How to Influence and Lead Others Efficiently and Effectively

Provides the range of leadership alternatives, and overcomes the focus on a "perfect style." Uses practical variables such as time management, subordinate development, commitment and quality to help determine which styles are best in what circumstances. Debunks the esoteric notions of vision and lofty mission statements, and provides prac-tical help for leadership every day with customers, employees, vendors and the public.

Ordering information on page 51.

ALAN WEISS

Alan Weiss is the founder and president of Summit Consulting Group, Inc., a firm specializing in management and organization development. Summit's clients include organizations such as Merck & Co., Hewlett-Packard, GE, National Westminster Bank, The New York Times, Mercedes-Benz, the American Press Institute, the American Institute of Architects, Coldwell Banker and over 80 other organizations in four countries.

Alan has published over 300 articles in the fields of strategy, innovation, leadership, ethics, diversity, and interpersonal relations, in publications ranging from *Management Review* to *The New York Times*. He is the co-author of *The Innovation Formula* (1988: HarperCollins), and author of *Managing for Peak Performance* (1989: HarperCollins), *Making It Work* (1990: HarperCollins) and *Million Dollar Consulting* (1992: McGraw-Hill). All of his books have been alternate or main book club selections, and two have been translated into German and Italian. He has also authored the Professional Development Series Booklets on major management and self-improvement topics.

He appears frequently on radio and television interview programs to discuss productivity and quality. He is a member of the American Counseling Association and the American Management Association, and is the former president of the New England Speakers Association. He holds the designation "Certified Management Consultant" from the Institute of Management Consultants, the only accrediting body requiring client references, evidence of successful engagements, and completion of a sitting examination on ethical practices. He has earned the designation "Certified Speaking Professional" from the National Speakers Association, which has recognized fewer than 300 individuals at that level of performance.

Alan is the former president of Kepner-Tregoe Continuing Education, and vice president of Kepner-Tregoe, Inc., an international training firm, and the former CEO of Walter V. Clarke Associates, a behavioral consulting firm. He holds a bachelor's degree in political science from Rutgers University, masters degrees in political science from Montclair College and psychology from California Coast University, and a doctorate in psychology from California Coast University. He has traveled to 49 countries and 48 states in the course of his career. Success Magazine has cited him in an editorial devoted to his work as "a worldwide expert in executive education."

He once appeared on the popular TV game show *Jeopardy*, where he lost badly in the first round to a dancing waiter from Iowa.

In addition to his worldwide consulting work, Alan Weiss presents over 50 keynote addresses and workshops annually for management conferences, trade association conventions and public symposia. For more information on his topics and availability, contact Summit Consulting Group, Inc. at the address or toll-free number on page 51.

ORDERING INFORMATION

Please make your selections below and mail or fax this entire sheet to:

Summit Bookstore
Summit Consulting Group, Inc.
Box 1009
East Greenwich, RI 02818
Fax: 401/884-5068
Or place your order via credit card using our
toll-free number: 800/766-7935.
Checks, Visa, MasterCard and company purchase orders are all welcome.

Please see the reverse side for volume orders and other information.

Books	Cost	Number	Total
Million Dollar Consulting (soft cover)	$12.95	_____	$_____
Best Laid Plans (hard cover)	$22.50	_____	$_____
Managing for Peak Performance (hard cover)	$18.00	_____	$_____
The Innovation Formula (soft cover)	$9.95	_____	$_____
Cassettes			
Peak Performance Album (three tapes)	$33.95	_____	$_____
Booklets: The Professional Development Series			
How to Maximize Fees in Professional Services	$6.95	_____	$_____
Rejoicing in Diversity	$6.95	_____	$_____
Doing Well by Doing Right	$6.95	_____	$_____
Raising the Bar	$6.95	_____	$_____
Leadership Every Day	$6.95	_____	$_____
Volume order from reverse side			$_____
Subtotal			$_____
Rhode Island only, add 7% sales tax			$_____
Shipping: $2.90 per item (free shipping for three or more items)			$_____
Total			$_____

Payment by ❑ check   ❑ purchase order, number:_____

❑ Visa   ❑ MasterCard, number: _____ exp:_____

Signature: _____ Phone:_____

Name: _____Title:_____

Organization: _____ _____

Address (City, State, Zip): _____ _____

ORDERING INFORMATION

Volume discounts are available on the Professional Development Series Booklets:

Units	Price Per Unit
1-99	$6.95
100-499	$6.45
500-999	$5.95
1000+	$5.45

You may order booklets in any combination of titles. We can also provide the booklets with your organization's logo, with a custom-designed introduction, or with a preface written by a company executive. Please call for details and charges.

Please send the following booklets in the quantities specified:

Title:	**Number:**
How to Maximize Fees in Professional Services	_____
Rejoicing in Diversity	_____
Doing Well by Doing Right	_____
Raising the Bar	_____
Leadership Every Day	_____
Total number ordered	_____
Price per unit above	$_____
Total price (Record on reverse side)	$_____

Shipping is free on quantity orders of three or more booklets. Use reverse side for orders of three or less.